Overview Fresh from the Farm!

Fruits and vegetables go from farm to market.

Reading Vocabulary Words

produce
temperature
transport

High-Frequency Words

fruits	*some*
fresh	*keep*
they	*grown*
picked	*place*

Building Future Vocabulary

* *These vocabulary words do not appear in this text. They are provided to develop related oral vocabulary that first appears in future texts.*

Words:	*stall*	*staple*	*process*
Levels:	Library	Library	Library

Comprehension Strategy
Sequencing ideas and story events

Fluency Skill
Pronouncing difficult words accurately

Phonics Skill
Using knowledge of vowel digraphs *ui* (fr<u>ui</u>ts, j<u>ui</u>cy), *ou* (f<u>ou</u>nd, h<u>ou</u>rs, wareh<u>ou</u>se)

Reading-Writing Connection
Making a chart

Home Connection
Send home one of the Flying Colors Take-Home books for children to share with their families.

Differentiated Instruction
Before reading the text, query children to discover their level of understanding of the comprehension strategy — Sequencing ideas and story events. As you work together, provide additional support to children who show a beginning mastery of the strategy.

Focus on ELL

- Assemble photographs of fruits and vegetables. Help children associate them with the correct English terms.

- Have children arrange the photographs in a bulletin board display of farm produce and help them make labels identifying each fruit and vegetable.

T1

Using This Teaching Version

1. Before Reading

2. During Reading

3. Revisiting the Text

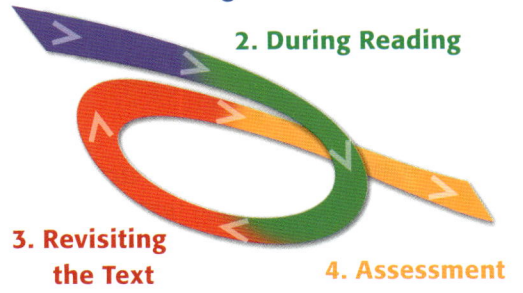

4. Assessment

This Teaching Version will assist you in directing children through the process of reading.

1. **Begin with Before Reading** to familiarize children with the book's content. Select the skills and strategies that meet the needs of your children.

2. **Next, go to During Reading** to help children become familiar with the text, and then to read individually on their own.

3. **Then, go back to Revisiting the Text** and select those specific activities that meet children's needs.

4. **Finally, finish with Assessment** to confirm children are ready to move forward to the next text.

1 Before Reading

Building Background
- Write the word *produce* on the board. Read it aloud. Ask children to name things they might see in the produce section of a grocery store.
- Introduce the book by reading the title, talking about the cover photograph, and sharing the overview.

Building Future Vocabulary
Use Interactive Modeling Card: Meaning Map
- Write *stall* in the Word box. Look through the book to find picture clues of produce *stall*s. Have children write a sentence in the Sentence box and suggest a definition of *stall* based on the clues.
- Model using a dictionary to find the definition that applies in this context and write it on the Meaning Map. Ask children to help you write a sentence that shows this meaning of the word.

Introduction to Reading Vocabulary
- On blank cards write: *produce*, *transport*, and *temperature*. Read them aloud. Tell children these words will appear in the text of *Fresh from the Farm!*
- Use each word in a sentence for understanding.

Introduction to Comprehension Strategy

- Explain that authors present information in an order, or sequence. Say *Authors often tell about events in the order they happened, or they tell the steps of a task in the order the steps should be completed.*
- Tell children that they will be reading about the sequence of events that brings fruits and vegetables from farms to markets.
- Ask *Where do you buy the fruits and vegetables that you eat?*

Introduction to Phonics

- Write *ui* and *ou* on the board and explain that a vowel digraph is two vowels working as a team to make a sound.
- Write **fruits** and **juicy** on the board. Read the words aloud. Point out that in these words the *ui* digraph makes the long /u/ sound. Write **found** and **hours** on the board. Read the words aloud. Point out that in these words the *ou* digraph makes the /ow/ sound.
- Have children practice saying **fruits** and **juicy,** and then **found** and **hours.**

Modeling Fluency

- Read the first paragraph on page 3 aloud. Point out that readers might have difficulty pronouncing some of the words, such as *vitamins, minerals,* and *diseases.*
- Model sounding out the words *vitamins* and *minerals*. Point out that knowing the sounds vowel digraphs make can also help us pronounce unfamiliar words. Talk about other tools for pronouncing difficult words, including root words, prefixes, suffixes, word families, and dictionaries.

2 During Reading

Book Talk
Beginning on page T4, use the During Reading notes on the left-hand side to engage children in a book talk. On page 24, follow with Individual Reading.

T3

During Reading

Book Talk
- Ask children to look at the cover photograph and name as many of the fruits and vegetables as they can. Ask *Have you eaten any of these fruits or vegetables in the past week? Which ones?*

- **Comprehension Strategy**
Point to the table of contents and explain that it lists the parts of the book in sequence. Ask *What is the name of the first chapter?* ("Good Food, Healthy Food") *What is the name of the next chapter?* ("Buying Fruits and Vegetables") *What follows the last chapter?* (glossary and index)

- Hold up the word card for *produce*. Have children find the word in the table of contents and practice saying it. Say *Produce means farm crops, especially fresh fruits and vegetables.*

Turn to page 2 – Book Talk

Revisiting the Text

Fresh from the Farm!

Heather Hammonds

Contents

Chapter 1	Good Food, Healthy Food	2
Chapter 2	Buying Fruits and Vegetables	4
Chapter 3	Down on the Farm	6
Chapter 4	Keeping Produce Fresh	8
Chapter 5	To Market, To Market!	12
Chapter 6	Straight to the Supermarket	14
Chapter 7	Best Bananas	16
Chapter 8	Fresh Produce from Far Away	18
Chapter 9	Fresh Produce from Close to Home	20
Chapter 10	Follow the Fresh Produce Trail	22
Glossary and Index		24

Future Vocabulary

- Reread the book title and remind children that this book is about fresh fruits and vegetables, which are also called produce. Say *Farmers also grow grain, rice, and other staple crops.* Explain that staple crops are often sold in large quantities to companies that make flour, bread, cereal, and other important basic foods.

- Ask children to think of another kind of staple that they might find in a desk drawer. (staples for fastening sheets of paper together)

Now revisit pages 2–3

During Reading

Book Talk

- Point out that the word *diet* is printed in boldfaced type. Explain that this means the word is included in the glossary. Ask children to look up *diet* in the glossary.

- Ask children to name the fruits and vegetables in the photograph at the top of page 3. *(bell peppers, kumquats, banana, mushroom, orange, tomato, carrot, lemon, apple)*

- **Phonics Skill** Remind children that the digraph *ou* makes the /ow/ sound in *found* and *hours.* Ask them to find another word on these pages where the *ou* digraph makes the /ow/ sound. *(our)* Ask them to find words where the *ou* digraph makes a different sound. *(should, four)*

Turn to page 4 — Book Talk

Chapter 1

Good Food, Healthy Food

Fruits and vegetables are the parts of plants that can be eaten. Many fruits are sweet and juicy and have seeds.

Raw, uncooked vegetables are crisp and crunchy. Both fruits and vegetables are part of a healthy **diet**.

2

Revisiting the Text

Fruits and vegetables contain lots of **vitamins** and **minerals** to keep our bodies healthy and strong. Eating fruits and vegetables helps protect us against some diseases, too.

Fruits and vegetables can be fresh, frozen, canned, or dried. Children should eat three to four cups of fruits and vegetables every day!

Cut, peeled, or broken-apart fresh fruits and vegetables should be stored in the refrigerator.

Future Vocabulary

- Ask children to name fruits and vegetables that they sometimes eat fresh and uncooked. (apples, bananas, oranges, tomatoes, carrots, celery, onions) Explain that produce that is not going to be eaten quickly must be processed in some way, such as freezing, canning, or drying. Ask children to give examples of processed fruits and vegetables their family uses. (frozen peas, canned fruit juice, dried raisins)

Now revisit pages 4–5

During Reading

Book Talk

- Ask *Which word on these pages is included in the glossary? (grocery) How do you know?* (It is printed in boldfaced type.)

- Hold up the word card for *transport*. Have children find a form of the word on these pages and practice saying it. *(transported)*

- Talk about the kinds of places where fruits and vegetables are sold. Ask volunteers to tell about their own experiences going to a small grocery store, supermarket, farmers' market, or roadside stand. Ask *Has your family ever shopped for produce on a Web site?*

Turn to page 6 — Book Talk

Chapter 2

Buying Fruits and Vegetables

Fruits and vegetables are sold at small **grocery** stores, large supermarkets, local farmers' markets, and roadside stands. They are also sold on Web sites!

Where do these places get the fruits and vegetables to sell?

4

Revisiting the Text

How are fruits and vegetables transported to stores and markets?

How are they kept fresh while they are transported?

Turn the page to learn more!

Fruits and vegetables are also called produce.

Future Vocabulary

- Remind children of the Meaning Map completed earlier. Invite them to look closely at the produce stalls in the photograph and identify some of the fruits and vegetables they see. Ask *What could be the purpose of the awning, or cloth roof, over the stalls?* (to keep the people and the produce cooler, to keep rain or dust off the produce)

Now revisit pages 6–7

During Reading

Book Talk

- Ask *Which words on these pages are included in the glossary?* (climates, harvested, damaged)

- **Comprehension Strategy**
  Ask *How has the author sequenced, or ordered, the information in Chapter 3?* (in the order events happen) *What happens first, even before planting?* (The farmer learns about the climate and soil.) *What happens next?* (planting) *Next?* (growing) *Next?* (harvesting) *What sometimes happens even after the* produce *is picked?* (Some fruits and vegetables continue to ripen.)

Turn to page 8 — Book Talk

Chapter 3

Down on the Farm

Fruits and vegetables are grown on farms. Before planting, farmers need to know what types of plants grow best in their **climates** and soils.

After planting, many fruits and vegetables take several months, or longer, to grow. Apple trees take four to five years to produce their first fruit!

apples

lettuce

6

Revisiting the Text

When fruits and vegetables are ready to be **harvested**, they are picked very carefully. **Damaged** produce spoils quickly and cannot be sold or eaten.

Farmers have to know when to pick their crops. Many fruits and vegetables continue to ripen after they are picked.

Many fruits and vegetables are picked by hand, but some are harvested with machines.

Future Vocabulary
- **Comprehension Strategy**
  Explain that the word *process* also means a step-by-step way to complete a task or reach a goal. Say *In Chapter 3 the author begins explaining the process that brings us fresh fruits and vegetables. What is the first step in the process?* (The farmer studies climate and soil.) *What is the next step?* (planting) *What step in the process is shown in the photograph on page 7?* (picking, harvesting)

Now revisit pages 8–9

During Reading

Book Talk
- Hold up the word card for *temperature*. Have children find the word on these pages and practice saying it together and individually. If there is a thermostat in your classroom, check it to find out the *temperature*.

- **Phonics Skill** Remind children that the digraph *ui* makes the long /u/ sound in *fruits* and *juicy*. Ask them to find a word where the *ui* digraph makes a different sound. *(quickly)*

- **Comprehension Strategy**
Say *This chapter tells some of the things that happen after the produce is picked.* Think aloud with children about this sequence of events. Encourage them to use vocabulary that signals sequencing, such as *next, then,* and *before*.

Turn to page 10 – Book Talk

Chapter 4

Keeping Produce Fresh

Fresh produce is usually sorted and packed after picking.

Some fruits and vegetables are sorted into different sizes or colors. Then they are packed into boxes.

Apples and potatoes can be kept for many weeks after picking.

Peaches and peas only stay fresh for about two weeks.

8

Revisiting the Text

Packed fruits and vegetables are placed in special rooms. The temperature in these rooms can be controlled.

Fruits and vegetables must be cooled quickly after they are picked. Cool temperatures help keep produce fresh.

32°F   57°F

Different fruits and vegetables are kept at different temperatures.

Future Vocabulary
- Ask *What step in the process is shown in the photograph on page 8?* (packing) *What step in the process is shown in the photograph at the top of page 9?* (storage in temperature-controlled rooms)

Now revisit pages 12–13

During Reading

Book Talk

- **Comprehension Strategy** Ask children to look at the photograph on page 10 and tell what is happening. (The tomatoes are being washed in water to cool them off.) Ask *When do the tomatoes get washed?* Return to pages 8–9 for clues. Think aloud about how the author sequenced the information about cooling the produce. Ask *Could the author have put this information in a different place?* (yes, at the beginning of the chapter)

- **Fluency Skill** Point out that some readers might have difficulty pronouncing *refrigerated.* Remind children that they know the prefix *re-* from many other words. Ask them to think of examples. *(redo, report)* Model sounding out the rest of the word letter by letter.

➡ *Turn to page 12 — Book Talk*

Some kinds of fresh produce are covered in ice after they have been picked. Others are washed in water.

This helps cool them quickly.

Refrigerated trucks are used to transport fresh produce from the farms.

Machines keep the inside of the trucks cool. The fruits and vegetables stay fresh as they are moved from place to place.

The walls of refrigerated trucks are lined with special materials that help keep the inside temperature cool.

During Reading

Book Talk

- **Phonics Skill** Ask children to find words on these pages where the *ou* digraph makes the /ow/ sound as in the word *hours*. *(found, amount, around)*

- **Fluency Skill** Say *Sometimes if I can't decide how to pronounce a difficult word, I look it up in a dictionary.* Model looking up *restaurant* and point out that more than one pronunciation is given. Explain that some words are pronounced differently by different people, for example, people who live in different areas.

- **Comprehension Strategy** Use the photographs to talk about the sequence of events in this chapter.

Turn to page 14 – Book Talk

Chapter 5
To Market, To Market!

Some fresh produce is transported from farms to big markets. These markets sell the produce to people who own stores and **restaurants**.

The produce is stored in **temperature-controlled** rooms until it is sold. Big markets are found in cities all around the world.

12

Revisiting the Text

Big markets open very early in the morning.

Buyers from grocery stores and restaurants look at the produce carefully. They choose the fruits and vegetables that they will sell in their stores or will serve in their restaurants.

The people buy just the amount of produce they think they can sell or use. Produce does not stay fresh for a long time.

Many restaurant cooks plan their meals around the produce they buy at the market.

Future Vocabulary
- Ask children if they can think of other kinds of stalls besides produce stalls. Talk about stalls for animals in barns or stables, parking stalls for automobiles, and shower stalls.

Now revisit pages 16–17

During Reading

Book Talk

- **Fluency Skill** Point out that some readers might have trouble pronouncing the word *distribution.* Sound out the first part of the word letter by letter. Then talk about how the familiar suffix *-ion* can help a reader finish pronouncing the word. On the board, write other words that end in *-ion,* such as *action, lotion,* and *promotion.* Say the words aloud.

- **Comprehension Strategy** Write these words signaling sequence on the board: *first, next, then, before, after, finally.* Ask volunteers to retell events on these pages using the signal words.

Turn to page 16 – Book Talk

Chapter 6

Straight to the Supermarket

Most of the fruits and vegetables grown on farms are sold to big company supermarkets. There can be hundreds of supermarkets that belong to the same company and have the same name.

Refrigerated trucks take fresh produce to supermarket **distribution centers.**

The fresh produce is kept at the distribution centers.

Each of the supermarket's stores puts in orders for fruits and vegetables. Then the fruits and vegetables are taken to the stores.

Supermarkets keep all their goods at distribution centers before they are taken to the supermarket's stores.

During Reading

Book Talk

- **Comprehension Strategy** Ask *Are bananas picked before or after they are ripe?* (before) *When are bananas covered with special bags?* (while they grow) *Are bananas ripened before or after they are transported to the warehouse?* (after)

- Talk to children about how the ripening process continues. Ask *How do bananas usually look and feel at the time we buy them?* (yellow, sometimes with green parts, firm) *How do they change as they sit on the kitchen counter?* (They get brown spots; they get soft.) *Do the taste and smell of the bananas change?* Model using words signaling sequence as you talk and encourage children to use these words.

Turn to page 18 – Book Talk

Chapter 7

Best Bananas

These bananas are grown on a big banana **plantation**. They are picked before they are ripe. This helps keep them fresh longer. They are packed in boxes and kept in a cool room.

Bananas are covered with special bags while they grow. This keeps them clean and makes them grow faster.

16

Revisiting the Text

The green bananas are transported to a big **warehouse**. They are kept in ripening rooms.

Special gas is pumped into the rooms to make the bananas ripen.

Future Vocabulary

- Say *I learned some interesting things about the process of growing bananas and getting them to market. Did you?* Talk about the special bags that cover bananas while they grow, the fact that bananas are picked before they are ripe, and the special gas that is used to make bananas ripen in the warehouse.

Now revisit pages 18–19

During Reading

Book Talk

- **Phonics Skill** Remind children that the digraph *ou* sometimes makes the /ow/ sound as in the words *hours* and *found.* Ask them to find words on these pages where the *ou* digraph makes other sounds. *(countries, country, bought)*

- **Fluency Skill** Talk about how readers pronounce difficult words by breaking them down into pieces. Write *exporting* and *importing* on the board, breaking each into its prefix *(ex-, im-),* root word *(port),* and suffix *(-ing).* Model sounding out each word piece by piece.

Turn to page 20 – Book Talk

Chapter 8

Fresh Produce from Far Away

Some of the fresh produce sold in stores or used in restaurants is grown in other countries.

Fruits and vegetables are transported quickly in refrigerated trucks, trains, ships, or airplanes.

18

Revisiting the Text

Some fruits, like bananas, only grow in warm places. Countries where it is too cold to grow bananas get all their bananas from warmer countries.

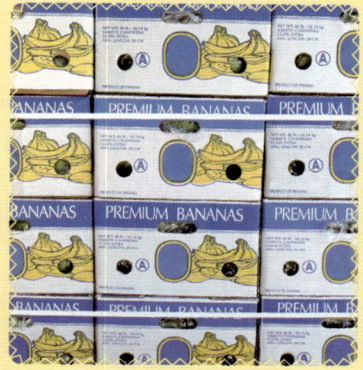

Some countries get lots of fresh produce from other countries!

When goods are sold to another country, it is called *exporting*. When goods are bought from another country, it is called *importing*.

19

Future Vocabulary
- Tell children that *stall* also means to stop or to delay something. Ask *Why would it be bad to stall the shipment of produce from one country to another?* (The fruits and vegetables must be transported quickly so that they stay fresh.)

Now revisit pages 20–21

19

During Reading

Book Talk

- **Comprehension Strategy**
  Ask *Has anyone ever visited a farmers' market?* Encourage children to tell about their experiences in time order. Prompt them with questions. Ask *When did your outing begin? What did you see or buy first at the market? What kinds of produce did you see there? What other things were for sale at the farmers' market?* (flowers, baked goods, animals, eggs, crafts) *After you looked around a while, did you take a break to get something to eat or drink? What did you do after you finished shopping?*

Turn to page 22 – Book Talk

Chapter 9

Fresh Produce from Close to Home

a farmers' market

We can buy fresh produce from other countries. We can also buy fresh produce that has been grown close to where we live.

Small markets, called farmers' markets, are found in many cities and towns.

20

Revisiting the Text

Farmers bring their fresh produce to the farmers' market nearest to them. Visitors to the farmers' market buy the fresh produce straight from the farmer. Sometimes the produce is sold just hours after it was picked.

Some farmers let you pick your own fruits and vegetables before you buy them.

Future Vocabulary
- Explain that at the farmers' market, the farmer's whole family may help out at their produce stall. Say *Some regular visitors to the farmers' market get to know the farmers who grow the fruits and vegetables. Why might it be better to buy produce from someone you know rather than in a big supermarket?*

Now revisit pages 22–23

During Reading

Book Talk

- Leave this page spread for children to discover on their own when they read the book individually.

Turn to page 24 – Book Talk

Chapter 10

Follow the Fresh Produce Trail

These delicious apples are:

- harvested
- packed and kept in a cool room
- transported to a distribution center 
- transported to large supermarkets
- sold to you! 

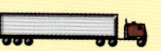

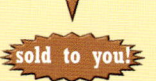

22

Revisiting the Text

These delicious peaches are:

harvested

↓

packed and kept in a cool room

↓

transported to a wholesale market

↓

sold to a small grocery store

↓

sold to you!

23

Future Vocabulary
- Say *The fresh produce trails for these apples and peaches both begin with the harvest. What other steps in the process are the same for the apples and peaches?* (Both are packed and kept in a cool room.) *How is the process different for apples and peaches?* (The apples are transported to a distribution center and then to a large supermarket; the peaches are transported to a wholesale market and then sold to a small grocery store.)

Go to page T5 — Revisiting the Text

During Reading

Book Talk
- Note: Point out this text feature page as a reference for children's use while reading independently.

Individual Reading
Have each child read the entire book at his or her own pace while remaining in the group.

Go to page T5 – Revisiting the Text

Glossary

climate	the type of weather in a certain place
damaged	injury or hurt that lessens the value of something
diet	the food and drink you usually eat
distribution center	a warehouse where goods are kept before being transported to other places
grocery	a small store that sells food and things for the house
harvested	picked after the growing season is over
minerals	important parts in food that are necessary for bodies to be healthy and strong
restaurants	places to buy and eat meals
temperature-controlled	kept at certain level or temperature
vitamins	important parts in food that are necessary for bodies to be healthy and strong
warehouse	a large building where goods are kept

Index

bananas 16–17, 19
diet 2
distribution centers 14–15, 22
farmers' markets 4, 20–21
farms 6, 11–12, 14

refrigerated trucks 11, 14, 18
supermarkets 4, 14–15, 22
wholesale markets 12–13

24

During independent work time, children can read the online book at:
www.rigbyflyingcolors.com

3 Revisiting the Text

Future Vocabulary
- Use the notes on the right-hand pages to develop oral vocabulary that goes beyond the text. These vocabulary words first appear in future texts. These words are: *stall*, *staple*, and *process*.

Turn back to page 1

Reading Vocabulary Review
Activity Sheet: New Word Log

- Have children write *produce* in the New Word column. Ask them to write the meaning in the second column and to write why the author might have chosen this word in the third column.
- Have each child select additional words from the book to complete the New Word Log.

Comprehension Strategy Review
Use Interactive Modeling Card: Making Your Own Judgment

- Write a thought-provoking fact from the book in the first column. Think aloud as you make a judgment about this fact. Model finding support in the book for your judgment.
- Invite children to help make additional judgments based on the reading.

Phonics Review
- On the board, write the following words: *fruits, juicy, found, hours,* and *warehouse.*
- Have volunteers underline the vowel digraph in each word and pronounce the word.

Fluency Review
- Read aloud page 3, reviewing the pronunciation of the words *vitamins, minerals, diseases,* and *refrigerator* and clues for decoding difficult words.
- Partner children and have them read page 3. Encourage children to help each other pronounce difficult words.

Reading-Writing Connection
Activity Sheet: Story Sequence Chart

To assist children with linking reading and writing:

- Ask children to write the title of Chapter 7 at the top of the Story Sequence Chart and then fill in the Beginning, Middle, and End boxes with three sequential events described in the chapter.
- Have children draw and label a chart similar to those on pages 22–23 to show the produce trail from the farm to the farmers' market and the buyer.

4 Assessment

Assessing Future Vocabulary
Work with each child individually. Ask questions that elicit each child's understanding of the Future Vocabulary words. Note each child's responses:

- Where would you find a vegetable stall, at a market or in a garden?
- Which of these is a staple crop: peaches, wheat, or lettuce?
- When you brush your teeth, what is the first step in the process?

Assessing Comprehension Strategy
Work with each child individually. Note each child's understanding of sequencing ideas and story events:

- Starting at the farm, name three things that might happen to an apple before it gets to you.
- Use the words *first, next,* and *then* to tell how to make your favorite sandwich.
- Tell how produce gets from the market to the cooks at restaurants.

Assessing Phonics
Work with each child individually. Make word cards for *fruits, juicy, quickly, found, hours, warehouse, you,* and *countries.* Have each child identify the words where the vowel digraph *ou* makes the /ow/ sound. Then have each child find the words where the vowel digraph *ui* makes the long /u/ sound. Have each child read each word aloud. Note each child's responses for understanding the vowel digraphs *ou* and *ui*:

- Did each child recognize where the vowel digraph *ou* makes the /ow/ sound?
- Did each child recognize where the vowel digraph *ui* makes the long /u/ sound?
- Did each child accurately pronounce the words on the word cards?

Assessing Fluency
Have each child read page 3 to you. Note each child's understanding of pronouncing difficult words accurately:

- Was each child able to accurately pronounce all the words on the page?
- Did each child employ specific skills for decoding difficult words?

Interactive Modeling Cards

Meaning Map

stall	Stores display their produce in stalls.
Word	Sentence

I think the word means: sections where different fruits and vegetables are sold

The definition I found: a booth, stand, or counter at which items for sale are displayed

A new sentence that shows the meaning: Each stall at the farmers' market sold different fruits and vegetables.

Making Your Own Judgment

Story Event or Nonfiction Fact	Judgment	Support for Judgment
We can buy produce from many places.	We should buy more from farmers' markets.	Farmers' markets sell fresh, local produce.
Refrigerated trucks transport produce.	Trucks make supermarkets possible.	Produce needs to stay cool to stay fresh.

Directions: With children, fill in the Meaning Map using the word *stall* and picture clues from the text.

Directions: With children, fill in the Making Your Own Judgment chart for *Fresh from the Farm!*

Discussion Questions

- Why are some kinds of fresh produce covered in ice after they have been picked? (Literal)
- Which are stored at the cooler temperature after packing, peaches or bananas? (Critical Thinking)
- Why are more kinds of produce available in markets today than in the past? (Inferential)

Activity Sheets

New Word Log

New Word	Meaning in the Book	Why I Think the Author Chose the Word
produce	fresh fruits and vegetables	The fruits and vegetables are produced on the farm.
super-market	a large company market	*Super* makes me think of something big.
climate	the type of weather in a certain place	This is a scientific word.

Directions: Have children fill in the New Word Log using the word *produce* and additional words they choose from the text.

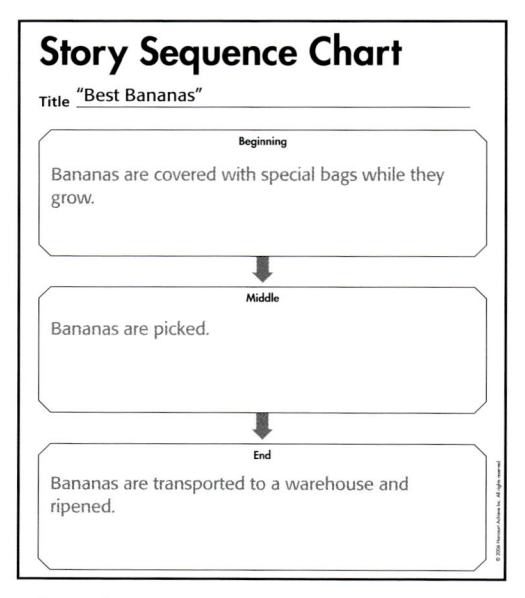

Story Sequence Chart

Title "Best Bananas"

Beginning
Bananas are covered with special bags while they grow.

Middle
Bananas are picked.

End
Bananas are transported to a warehouse and ripened.

Directions: Have children fill in the Story Sequence Chart for Chapter 7 of *Fresh from the Farm!*

Optional: On a separate sheet of paper, have children make a produce trail from the farm to the farmers' market and the buyer.